D0618342

EXPRESSING THE INNER

WILD

TATTOOS, PIERCINGS, JEWELRY, AND OTHER BODY ART

STEPHEN G. GORDON

TFCB

TWENTY-FIRST CENTURY BOOKS / MINNEAPOLIS

Twenty-First Century Books
A division of Lerner Publishing Group, Inc.
241 First Avenue North
Minneapolis, MN 55401 U.S.A.

For reading levels and more information, look up this title at www.lernerbooks.com.

Main Text font set in Fellbridge Std. 9.5/15.
Typeface provided by Monotype Typography.

The Cataloging-in-Publication Data for *Expressing the Inner Wild* is on file at the Library of Congress.

ISBN 978–1–4677–1467–9 (lib. bdg. : alk. paper)
ISBN 978–1–4677–2548–4 (eBook)

Manufactured in the United States of America
1 – PC – 12/31/13

contents

bling
FOREVER

SHE WEARS A LONG BLACK WIG TOPPED BY A GOLDEN, VULTURE-SHAPED HELMET. On top of that is a flat crown, with two enormous golden feathers projecting high into the air. A cobra-shaped earring curls through her earlobe, and heavy black makeup outlines her eyes.

Her companion also has a black wig, this one encircled by a red ribbon. She too wears a crown: a giant orange disk framed by cow horns, with a curled cobra hanging off the front. A striped, multicolored collar adorns her chest and shoulders, with matching bands around her upper and lower arms. Her eyes, too, are thickly rimmed with black eyeliner.

Who are these blinged-out celebrities? Rihanna and Beyoncé? Or maybe Nicki Minaj and Lady Gaga?

Nope. These bling sisters have nothing to do with pop music or show business. They've never even held a microphone or been on camera. These two are ancient—as in *three-thousand-years-ago* ancient. They are Queen Nefertari and the Goddess Isis. To people in ancient Egypt, they were big stars. And like all good celebrities, they liked their bling.

Which just goes to show you: body decoration has been in fashion for thousands of years. And thousands of years in the future, it will probably still be in fashion.

What makes people around the world want to beautify their bodies— from the tops of their heads to the tips of their toenails? What are the hottest trends? Let's find out.

Above: Queen Nefertari was the wife of Rameses II, who ruled ancient Egypt from 1279 BCE to 1213 BCE. This section of a mural in the queen's tomb shows her *(left)* with the mythical goddess Isis *(right). Left:* Thousands of years later, pop star Lady Gaga takes some of her style cues, including heavy eye makeup, from the ancient world.

CHAPTER 1

ALL THAT glitters

EVERY YEAR, AMERICANS BUY ABOUT $30 BILLION WORTH OF JEWELRY AT RETAIL STORES.

That's thirty *billion with a b* worth of necklaces, earrings, finger rings, brooches, and bracelets. Americans spend even more purchasing one-of-a-kind jewelry at art fairs and through handmade marketplaces such as Etsy.com. If you include toe rings, knuckle rings, and belly button rings, the dollar amount climbs higher. That's a lot of bling.

When we think of jewelry, we often think of metal-gem combos—a diamond set into a silver wedding ring, for instance, or a pair of gold earrings with emeralds. You'll see plenty of those at jewelry stores. But look around and you'll also see jewelry made of feathers, shells, leather, glass, plastic, and even telephone wire. Maybe you like to create your own jewelry, such as friendship bracelets made from yarn, string, and beads. One artist in Wisconsin makes necklaces out of spare buttons. Artists in Missouri and Brazil fashion earrings and bracelets out of used soda can tabs. Another artist, in the European country of Bulgaria, crafts pins and bracelets out of old metal zippers. Talk about recycling!

WHY DO THEY WEAR IT?

Most people wear jewelry because they like how it looks—and how it makes them look. A big pair of hoop earrings can make a great haircut look even better. A dangling navel ring can turn heads at a party. A big-and-bold knuckle ring says you have attitude. But reasons for wearing jewelry go deeper than good looks and flair.

Do you know men who wear wedding bands? A wedding ring sends a message. It tells anyone who might be looking for a mate that these guys are already spoken for. A glittery diamond on a woman's ring finger means that she's engaged to be married. She'll add a wedding band to that finger at the altar. In the song "Single Ladies," pop singer Beyoncé tells young men not to miss their chance. If a guy loves a girl, Beyoncé advises, he should make his love official with an engagement ring.

Many people wear jewelry to show what they believe in. A Christian might wear a small cross on a neck chain. A Jewish person might wear a chain with a Star of David. Other people wear little hearts to stand for love, or four-leaf clovers and horse- shoes as good luck charms. Some people don't bother with signs and symbols. They wear jewelry

Opposite: When combined with the sale of watches, yearly retail sales of jewelry in the United States top $70 billion each year. *Right:* In one popular song, Beyoncé sings about engagement rings. Her own style is flashy yet elegant.

THE KING OF BLING

Rapper Kanye West is known as a flashy dresser, and that flash extends to his jewelry. At the Black Entertainment Television Awards in 2010, Kanye decked himself out in $300,000 worth of jewelry. Around his neck hung a giant gold charm on a giant gold chain. The charm was shaped like the falcon-headed god Horus, the ancient Egyptian god of the sky. On his left hand, Kanye wore a four-finger gold knuckle ring adorned with two big gold pyramids. They looked like the pyramids where ancient Egyptians buried their dead kings. Kanye wore the jewelry while performing his song "Power." He wanted to show that he was powerful, like the ancient Egyptian gods and kings.

Later that same year, Kanye took his jewelry to a new level. He had a grille of gold and diamonds permanently affixed to his bottom teeth. Many other rappers and celebrities, including Olympic swimming star Ryan Lochte, have similar mouth jewelry. But unlike Kanye, most people who wear mouth jewelry simply slip the grille over their teeth. They don't have it attached permanently.

"I THINK SWAG IS VERY IMPORTANT TO RAPPERS. IT'S THE OVERALL APPEARANCE AND STYLE OF AN ARTIST— THESE BLUE SHORTS AND THIS BLUE HAT AND THIS $80,000 CHAIN, THIS JEWELRY AND ALL THESE TATTOOS, THAT'S SWAG."

—SOULJA BOY (LEFT), N.D.

printed with written messages so everyone knows where they stand. For example, if you see a girl with the words "never give up" printed on her wristband, you'll know that she's a fighter.

WHAT'S IT WORTH TO YOU?

Would you pay $9.7 million for a diamond? Maybe you wouldn't—but someone did. The Beau Sancy diamond sold at auction in May 2012 in Geneva, Switzerland, for almost $10 million! Why the high price tag? That diamond was worn by the queen of France at her coronation in 1610. It was later owned by British, Dutch, and Prussian royalty.

The British royal family has a vast collection of crown jewels. This treasure trove, which is displayed at the Tower of London in England, includes jewel-encrusted swords, scepters, and crowns. One of the crowns, the Imperial State Crown, is encrusted with almost three thousand diamonds, rubies, pearls, emeralds, sapphires, and other gemstones.

You don't have to spend a fortune to look like a king or a queen. You can buy a ring, a bracelet, or a necklace at the mall for less than twenty dollars. Jewelry made of inexpensive material is called costume jewelry.

You can also spend a lot more than twenty dollars on a piece of jewelry. People who own really expensive jewelry lock it up in vaults to keep it safe from thieves. Jewelry dealers ship diamonds and other valuable gems in armored trucks. The trucks are bulletproof and are staffed by armed guards.

Saint Edward's crown (named after an early English king) is the official coronation crown of the United Kingdom. It is made of solid gold and semiprecious stones. The crown has been worn by British kings and queens.

WHY BUY?

Imagine you're a movie star nominated for an Academy Award. You want to sparkle at the awards ceremony. You want to wear diamond earrings or a diamond necklace. Sure, you're a big movie star. You can afford expensive diamonds. But there's another option. Famous jewelers, such as Harry Winston of New York City, will rent jewelry just for the evening. You can save a bundle of money this way. If you're not a Hollywood star, you can still rent bling. Lots of online sites rent jewelry on a monthly basis or just for a special event.

But sometimes the best security measures are no match for thieves determined to steal expensive jewels. In February 2013, a team of eight gangsters, dressed as police officers, crashed through the gates of the Brussels Airport in Belgium in two vehicles. Acting quickly and waving guns, they stole around $50 million worth of jewels that had just been transferred from an armored truck into the cargo hold of an airplane.

'ROUND THE GLOBE

Imagine dressing yourself in jewelry from head to toe. If you were getting married in India, you might do just that. In addition to beautiful gowns and veils, some brides in India cover themselves in jewels. They drape jeweled head ornaments in their hair and fabulous jeweled chokers around their necks. They put on big, showy earrings and lots of bangles, or bracelets. But the bling doesn't stop there. An Indian bride might wear jeweled hand ornaments on her wrists and her fingers, not to mention finger rings, thumb rings, and even toe rings. She might wear beads and bells around her waist and anklets above her feet.

A bejeweled bride at her wedding ceremony in India

Why does an Indian bride wear all this jewelry? This custom is related to India's ancient tradition of jewelry making, dating back at least five thousand years. In addition, in Indian society, certain gemstones and precious metals symbolize wealth, health, and good fortune.

Almost everywhere on Earth, people wear jewelry. In East Africa, young women sometimes drape more than sixty strands of beads around their necks—from their chins down to their shoulders. In Turkey many people wear charms made of thick blue glass, with an eyeball decoration in the center. The charms are supposed to ward off the evil eye (harmful spirits). In China people believe that jade brings good luck, so Chinese people often wear jade jewelry.

In places with natural deposits of turquoise (the US Southwest, for instance), you'll find a lot of turquoise jewelry. In parts of South America and other places with rich deposits of silver, silver jewelry is common. At the same time, the world is at your fingertips. You might be able to walk into a gift shop in your neighborhood and buy earrings from India or bracelets from Mexico. If not, you can buy them online.

LONG AGO

Who were the first people to wear jewelry? No one knows the answer. But we do know that ancient people really liked their bling. The ancient Egyptians were a flashy bunch. Cornelian, lapis lazuli, jasper, amethyst, turquoise, alabaster, malachite, glass, ivory, gold, and silver—if it looked pretty or shiny, the ancient Egyptians used it to make jewelry. But this was not your ordinary costume jewelry from Claire's. This bling was expensive. Only ancient Egyptian kings, queens, and other rich and famous people could afford it. A common symbol on ancient Egyptian jewelry was the scarab, a type of beetle. The scarab was a symbol of resurrection, or life after death.

The center of the Inca Empire was in what is now Cuzco, Peru, near the mineral-rich Andes Mountains. When the Spanish conquered the region in the 1500s, they took vast amounts of the region's gold back to Spain, where most of it was melted down for coins. This gold Inca neck collar comes from the era before the Spanish conquest.

The Inca, who ruled a vast empire in South America in the 1400s and the 1500s, had a thing for gold. Gold was connected to Inti, the Inca sun god. Only the emperor (who was a descendant of Inti, according to Inca belief), nobles, and religious leaders were allowed to wear gold jewelry. Everyone else had to stick with copper, silver, and other materials. Inca nobles often wore big disk-shaped earrings called ear flares. Nose rings, bracelets, and giant neck collars were also common Inca jewelry.

Fashions in jewelry have changed over the course of human history, and fashions will continue to change. No one knows what jewelry of the future will look like, but as long as people have ears, necks, arms, fingers, and toes—and everything in between—they'll be loading up on jewelry.

CHAPTER 2

WILD hair

WHEN STARLETS GO TO AWARDS SHOWS, REPORTERS WONDER AHEAD OF TIME, "WHAT GOWNS WILL THEY WEAR?" But when rapper Nicki Minaj goes to an awards show, people ask, "What kind of hair will she wear?" You never know with Minaj. She might wear a giant bubblegum-pink updo. She might wear blue-green curls or long flame-orange locks. Or she might go for the rainbow look. Minaj loves to wear wigs—the bigger, crazier, and more colorful the better.

Hair is a built-in decoration. It can be styled in countless ways. You can braid it, curl it, straighten it, layer it, or decorate it with beads or glitter or flowers or jewels or feathers or bows—you name it! You can tie it up with a scarf. You can pile it up into a big beehive hairdo. Your hair isn't long enough? You can lengthen it with hair extensions. Don't like the color? You can dye it red or blond or black—or purple or green or pink. Or you can go the Nicki Minaj route and wig it.

Hairstyles go in and out of fashion. In the

1960s, many women wore tall, puffy bouffant hairdos. By the 1970s, that style was passé. Fast-forward forty years and bouffants were back. Many people look at fashion magazines before they go to the hairstylist. They might ask the stylist for bangs or a bob or a part down the middle, depending on the latest fashion trends.

ROCK 'N' ROLL LOCKS

Some people want a haircut that makes them look like a movie star. Others want a haircut that makes them look like a rock star. In 1964 the Beatles started a trend. Instead of the neatly clipped short hair worn by most males of that era, the four British rock 'n' rollers wore their hair long. It hung past their ears on the sides and touched their collars in back, with bangs over the forehead. Some adults were shocked, but teenage boys were thrilled. Soon millions of boys were sporting Beatles haircuts. Some boys didn't stop at their ears and collars. They grew their hair even longer. By the late 1960s, long hair was the sign of a full-fledged hippie—a young person who rebelled against social norms. The 1968 Broadway musical *Hair* celebrates the long-haired hippie scene of the 1960s.

The music–hair connection is still alive and well. Rocker Jimi Hendrix blazed a trail with his Afro. Punk rockers of the 1970s and the 1980s wore spiky Mohawks. Reggae singers sported dreadlocks. Hip-hop artists usually wear their hair super short. Some, like Lloyd, shave intricate designs into their short hair.

The Mohawk hairstyle dates back to ancient Ireland, Eurasia, and North Africa. Some Plains Indians of the Americas wore Mohawks, as did US paratroopers in World War II (1939–1945). In more recent years, Mohawks are often associated with punk rockers (*right*).

SCULPT HAIR

Like Nicki Minaj, pop singer Katy Perry loves to play with her hairstyle and hair colors. But her dye jobs pale in comparison to some of the hairdos on the recent cable show *Hair Battle Spectacular*. On this reality TV show, ten hair-stylists competed to create the most outrageous fantasy hair designs. They used a combination of real and artificial hair, along with wire, foam, props, and paints, to build hair sculptures on real people. Some sculptures looked

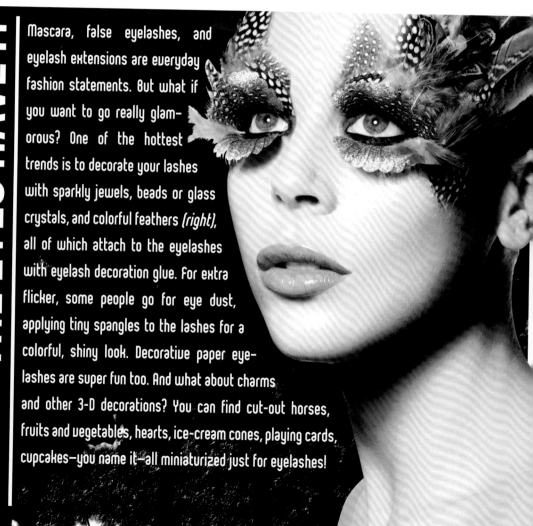

THE EYES HAVE IT

Mascara, false eyelashes, and eyelash extensions are everyday fashion statements. But what if you want to go really glamorous? One of the hottest trends is to decorate your lashes with sparkly jewels, beads or glass crystals, and colorful feathers *(right)*, all of which attach to the eyelashes with eyelash decoration glue. For extra flicker, some people go for eye dust, applying tiny spangles to the lashes for a colorful, shiny look. Decorative paper eyelashes are super fun too. And what about charms and other 3-D decorations? You can find cut-out horses, fruits and vegetables, hearts, ice-cream cones, playing cards, cupcakes—you name it—all miniaturized just for eyelashes!

like birds, poodles, wedding cakes, or houses. Others were abstract works of art. The winner of the contest—the one who made the most "hair dos" (as opposed to "hair don'ts")—won $100,000.

ABOUT FACE

Every year men from around the globe compete in the World Beard and Moustache Championships. The judges give awards in eighteen different categories, including the best Dalí mustache (a long pointy style made famous by Spanish painter Salvador Dalí); the best Amish beard (a full beard with no mustache); the best Fu Manchu (a long mustache that curves down alongside the mouth); and the best sideburns. In the freestyle categories, almost anything goes. Some contestants have giant curling mustaches. Others have beards down to their waists.

Facial hairstyles go in and out of fashion. Hip-hop star Ludacris, for instance, wears samurai-style sideburns, resembling those of historic Japanese warriors. Maybe you've seen actor Johnny Depp or musician Prince wearing a thin pencil mustache above the upper lip. That's not a brand-new style either. Many men wore pencil mustaches in the 1930s. Other facial hair trends include the goatee, a small pointed beard; and the soul patch, a little tuft of hair under the lower lip.

Willi Chevalier, from Germany, is a superstar of the beard and mustache world. An international champion, he is known for his black-and-white jackets and his "hair pretzel" beard and mustache.

THE WIDE WORLD OF HAIR

If you were to travel through the Guizhou Province in southern China, you might see women and girls with some really big hair. How big? How does 2 feet (0.6 meters) wide and 8 inches (20 centimeters) high grab you? That's the typical size of the hairdos of the Miao Long Horn women, members of an Asian ethnic group in China. To make this eye-catching hairstyle, a woman places a big curved piece of wood behind her head. She then wraps her own hair around the wood; adds extra hair saved from her mother, grandmothers, and great-grandmothers; and adds wool and linen to give the headdress more bulk. She keeps the whole thing in place with strips of white cloth. The final 'do looks like the horned head of a water buffalo or an oxen and is meant to honor these animals.

In contrast, the Masai women of eastern Africa shave their heads when they are old enough to marry. They wear beaded earrings, necklaces, and head-bands to make bald even more beautiful. Meanwhile, Masai men let their hair grow into long thick ropes, covering them with a paste of red ochre (a kind of iron ore). The long locks make the men look fierce.

Many popular hairstyles in the United States originated elsewhere. Cornrows, for instance, are an ancient style of braided hair that comes from West Africa. The braids,

Miao (or Hmong) women wrap white cord around the horns of their traditional hairstyle in a modified figure eight pattern.

worn by both men and women, can be left in place for weeks and are often decorated with colorful beads. Dreadlocks are closely linked to the Rastafarian religious group in Jamaica. Some Rastafarians grow dreads in accordance with a biblical passage that directs people not to cut their hair. People in other parts of the world wear dreads too. In India, for example, young women known as *devadasi* wear their hair in long matted dreads. The devadasi work in Hindu temples and devote their lives to the Hindu religion. Their hair is fashioned after images of long-haired Hindu goddesses.

Masai women typically shave their heads or wear their hair very short.

LONG AGO

Hairstyling has a long history. Archaeologists think that Stone Age people decorated their hair with clay, mud, and feathers. They probably made hairpins out of wood and animal bone. In the ancient cities of the Middle East, people used razors, tweezers, shaving mugs, and combs to comb and style their hair.

The ancient Egyptians were big wig wearers. Egyptian men generally shaved off their own hair, perhaps to keep their heads cool and clean. When they dressed up, they put on wigs made of human hair, wool, or the fibers of palm leaves. Most wigs were black, but some were dyed red, blue, or green. Many wigs had braids. Egyptian women also wore wigs—sometimes over a shaved head and sometimes over their own hair. The biggest wigs were reserved for the most important Egyptians.

"THE ACORNS OF THE FOREST OR THE WILD BEES OF THE HYBLA [A TOWN IN SICILY] CANNOT SURPASS IN NUMBER THE INFINITE VARIETY OF WOMEN'S COIFFURES."

—OVID, A ROMAN POET BORN IN THE FIRST CENTURY BCE

The ancient Greeks and Romans preferred their own hair to wigs. Men usually kept their hair short and simple. Roman women experimented with all kinds of hairstyles, from curls and topknots to ringlets and braids. They treated their hair with dyes, oils, and perfumes. They adorned it with ribbons, jeweled hairpins, flowers, pearls, and hairbands.

More than one thousand years ago, during the Heian era in Japan, many women grew their hair long—sometimes all the way to the floor. The style was straight and simple. In the following centuries, Japanese hairstyles got fancier. Women piled up their hair into big buns and held them in place with sticks and combs. They sometimes used wax to shape their hair into winglike formations. Women decorated their hair with jewels, ribbons, and flowers.

During the Edo period in Japan, from the 1600s through the late 1800s, noblemen warriors, or samurai, wore their hair in a style called *chonmage*, better known as a topknot. To create the chonmage, a man shaved the hair from the top of his head about halfway back. He pulled up the remaining hair into a ponytail and tied it flat on top of his head. The topknot helped keep a warrior's helmet from falling off during battle.

The squash blossom hairstyle is a jaw-dropping coiffure once worn by young Hopi women of the American Southwest. To make this style, a woman wound her hair into two big whorls, one on each side of the head. Young Hopi women adopted this style when they were old enough to marry and stopped wearing it after marriage.

CHAPTER 3

THE nail FILES

THE TYPICAL WOMAN'S FINGERNAIL MEASURES LESS THAN ONE-HALF INCH (1.25 CM) ACROSS. That's not much to work with—but to a fingernail artist, the nail's hard surface is a canvas for creating fabulous works of art.

Fingernail decoration can be a straightforward paint job. But for some people, a swipe of nail polish just isn't enough. They want stars and sparkles on their fingernails. Or maybe flowers or snowflakes or polka dots. Or stripes or leopard-skin spots.

Fingernail artists use different colors of polish, tiny brushes, colored markers, and other tools to create intricate designs on fingernails. Artists might use stamps to make identical designs from nail to nail. They might press glitter, decals, or tiny bits of foil onto nails and then cover them with top coat.

Pop star Rihanna is known for her glamorous nails. She has them done by top nail technicians such as Los Angeles-based Kimmie Kyees.

You can buy nail art kits and decorate your friends' nails at home. Or you can visit a local salon and have a trained manicurist make the artwork. Pop star Rihanna and supermodel Kate Moss aren't likely to trust their nails to the folks at the corner salon, though. When these stars want a special design, they visit famous fingernail artists such as Marian Newman and Jenny Longworth.

In 2011 a group of artists in London, England, staged an exhibit called Nailphilia. (The name means "nail love.") It was the first-ever art show dedicated to fingernail art. Most of the designs weren't very practical—imagine trying to type a homework assignment with a cluster of white and red roses cascading from your fingertips! But wow! They were eye-popping.

Most people who wear fingernail art are women and girls. But guys have started to get into the act too. Some decorate each nail to look like the head of a different comic book hero. Others might go with nails that look like LEGO tiles. And don't forget the toes. The big toe gives you more room for artistry than any of the fingernails. One man painted his big toes to look like a vampire's mouth with bloodred lips and fangs.

LONG, LONGER, LONGEST

Katy Perry has a thing for long fingernails. A set of golden nails she showed off in February 2011 were about 3 inches (7.5 cm) long! Of course, Perry didn't wait around for her nails to grow that long. Hers were false fingernails, attached with glue.

Some people take their time and grow long nails the old-fashioned way. In 2012 Chris "The Duchess" Walton, a singer from Las Vegas, Nevada, made the *Guinness World Records* for her fingernails, which measured 19 feet 9 inches (6 m) in length. It took Walton eighteen years to grow them that long. Previously, a woman from Salt Lake City, Utah, held the world's record with 28-foot (8.5 m) fingernails, but she broke them all in a car crash in 2009.

Chris Walton often paints her superlong nails to match her outfit. She says she doesn't have any trouble cooking, cleaning, playing the piano, or using the computer with her long nails.

"I DIDN'T GROW MY NAILS DELIBERATELY—I JUST STOPPED GETTING MANICURES AND STARTED TAKING CARE OF MY NAILS MYSELF. . . . I KEPT LIVING AND THEY KEPT GROWING."

—CHRIS WALTON, 2011

'ROUND THE WORLD

Sure, you can buy a bottle of nail polish for a few dollars. But some people make their own nail polish using all-natural materials. In South Korea, women mix up an orange paste using alum, a kind of salt, and the leaves and flowers of the *bong seon hwa* plant. (In English, the plant is called the garden balsam, rose balsam, or touch-me-not.) Korean women make the paste in the fall, after the rainy season ends, and use it to stain their fingernails. Eventually, though, the dye fades. Korean legend says that if a woman's fingernails are still orange by the time the snow falls in winter, she will marry her first love.

When it comes to fingernails, the Japanese don't hold back. In fact, some of the fingernail art in Japan is three-dimensional. People attach little plastic bows, figurines, flowers, jewels, and other charms to their nails. Nail art is impressive in Mexico too. Women's nails might have tiny decorative pieces that look like sliced fruit and flowers floating inside a shimmery clear coating.

Yoko Matsuda *(above)* is a popular nail artist in Japan. She specializes in 3-D designs, such as these Hello Kitty nails, which cost upward of $150 a set.

LONG AGO

Fingernail polish has a long history. It first appeared in China around 3000 BCE. People made a paste of plant gum, egg whites, gelatin, and beeswax, with the color coming from crushed-up roses and other flowers. The paste

FINGERNAIL BLING

Fergie and Beyoncé wear them. So do Lady Gaga and Rihanna and actress Rooney Mara. What are they? Fingernail rings! The rings slip easily over your fingertips and are an easy way to get a fun look. Some are even encrusted with diamonds and rubies and are valued as high as $36,000.

This Kathakali dancer from India wears traditional silver nail rings on the left hand. The classical art form, which combines music, dance, and drama, originated in the Indian state of Kerala in the 1600s.

dried into a hard lacquer. Wealthy Chinese nobles mixed bits of real gold or silver into the polish.

Chinese nobles—both men and women—frequently grew their fingernails long. Long nails were a status symbol in ancient China. They told everyone that you were rich. Since rich people had servants, long nails showed that you weren't working with your hands (which might break your long nails). The ancient Inca of South America decorated their fingernails too, often with pictures of gods and eagles. Cleopatra, an ancient Egyptian queen, wore red fingernails.

People in many other ancient cultures also painted their nails—many using henna-based paints. The decorative use of henna, a reddish-brown dye from

SPECIAL EFFECTS!

Magnetic nail polish is a fun polish technology. This polish has tiny metallic particles in it. After you apply the polish, while it's still wet, you hold a magnet over the polish. The magnet pulls the metal inside the polish into fabulous-looking stripes, curves, and other patterns. Once the polish is dry, you seal in the design by applying a layer of top coat.

the henna plant, was common among peoples living near the Mediterranean Sea, where the plant grows naturally. People in India and other parts of southern Asia also used henna to dye fingernails, hair, skin, and fabrics.

Painted fingernails stayed in fashion—primarily among upper-class women—through the centuries. A nail polish breakthrough came in the 1920s, when US chemists began to develop bright, strong, long-lasting paints for automobiles. Folks in the cosmetics industry quickly realized that similar chemical-based paints made great, long-lasting nail polish.

Gel nail polish is one of the latest developments in polish technology. Because of the special gels used to make the polish, it is stronger and lasts longer than other types of polish. Ordinary nail polish can begin to chip after a few days, while gel polish stays intact and shiny for several weeks. Getting a gel manicure is a bit more involved and more expensive than getting an ordinary nail job, however. You need to apply several layers of special undercoat before applying the top layer of polish. After application, you need to place your hands under ultraviolet (UV) light, which bakes the polish into your nails.

makeup
SENSATIONS

WHEN IT COMES TO MAKEUP, MOST PEOPLE DON'T GO WILD FOR SCHOOL OR A DAY AT THE OFFICE. They might turn up the volume for a night at a club or a party. If you really want to see people made up to the hilt, the best place to look is onstage. Performers are famous for their bold and colorful makeup. Lady Gaga is the queen of awesome makeup. In 2010 she attended a gala in New York with pearl-encrusted makeup. The next year, she appeared at the MTV Europe Music

"I JUST LOVE TO HAVE FUN AND BE EXPERIMENTAL WITH ALL SORTS OF THINGS. . . . I HAVE AN ATTRACTION TO UNIQUENESS."

—LADY GAGA *(RIGHT)*, 2012

Awards with shimmery blue lipstick, glittery green eyebrows, and swooping black eyeliner.

BOYS TOWN

If you think makeup is just for women and girls, think again. Eyeliner for men in ancient Egypt was not uncommon. In Europe in the Middle Ages, royal women—and men—covered scars and blemishes with face powder, rouge, and fake beauty marks.

Skip ahead to the 1950s, when early rock 'n' rollers such as Little Richard wore eyeliner and false eyelashes. Things really took off in the 1970s with David Bowie and other glam and glitter rockers, who applied colorful lipstick and bold eye makeup. The glam tradi-

Singer-songwriter-actor Adam Lambert is one of many male celebrities who wear makeup. In fact, Americans spent more than $5 billion in 2012 on men's grooming products. More than half was for skin care and cosmetics.

tion continues with men such as pop singer Adam Lambert, who often performs in black lipstick and dark eye makeup. Rock star Pete Wentz also wears a lot of guyliner.

Some of the most colorful men in makeup are drag performers—men who dress up like women for stage shows. First, the drag artist applies a heavy layer of pancake makeup to cover up facial hair and skin imperfections. (Pancake makeup comes out of the world of theater. It is a powder that is compressed into a flat "cake" and is typically applied with a damp sponge.) After applying the foundation, the drag artist puts on lipstick, eye shadow, eyeliner, blush, and false eyelashes. He piles on the bling in the hair and jewelry departments too. To see professional drag performers in action, tune in to *RuPaul's Drag Race*, a reality TV show on the Logo TV channel. On this show, hosted by the famous drag star RuPaul Charles, fourteen men compete for the title of America's Next Drag Superstar.

FAN BASE

Makeup artists generally work small. They use tiny brushes and pencils and pay precise attention to certain parts of the face: the eyes and the mouth in particular. But some people don't bother with all that precision. They treat

NOWHERE TO BE SEEN

In modern times, warriors sometimes paint their faces to blend in with their surroundings so they are difficult for the enemy to see. A soldier might use different shades of yellow and brown on the face to match the colors of the desert or green, black, and brown to match the colors of the forest. In fact, the word *camouflage* comes from the French verb *camoufler*, which means "to disguise."

An instructor in the Israeli army applies camouflage paint during a combat training course. Women in Israel's Defense Forces may serve in combat positions.

the entire face as a canvas and paint the whole thing in bold strokes with bold colors. A New York Jets fan might paint one side of her face green and the other side white—the team colors. And don't be surprised if you see a Dallas Cowboys fan with a giant blue star painted across his face. Some guys strip off their shirts and paint their whole chests and bellies with a team logo or team colors. Then they post their pictures on Pinterest!

'ROUND THE WORLD

The painted faces at sporting events look like amateur hour when compared to the face painting at the Goroka Show in Papua New Guinea, an island nation in the western Pacific Ocean. Every year in September, people from all over the island come to the town of Goroka to perform in a big cultural festival. More than one hundred groups take part. The participants dress in traditional tribal costumes. They sing, dance, and show off their age-old rituals.

The face and body painting at Goroka is fantastic. Each tribe has its own ancient designs. The Omo Masalai skeleton dancers, for instance, paint their faces to look like skulls and their bodies to look like skeletons. They paint white bones on their skin, corresponding to the real bones underneath, with the rest of their bodies painted black. The Huli Wigmen paint their faces bright red and yellow, accented with white lines and colored dots. Add enormous multicolored feathered headdresses, giant shell necklaces, grass skirts, and nose jewelry, and you've got a bling fest to rival anything else on Earth.

You can also see fantastic body painting in Africa. Among the Surma

> The Goroka Show in Goroka, Papua New Guinea, dates to the 1950s. About one hundred tribes take part, celebrating their music, dance, and culture. Face painting is one of the highlights.

HAND-TASTIC!

When some Indian women get married, they paint their hands and feet with henna dye, a tradition called *mehndi (right)*. The practice, a Hindu ritual, dates back thousands of years in India. It later spread to other parts of the world.

Mehndi artwork includes elaborate floral designs, paisley patterns, rows of circles and triangles, and other intricate designs. Mehndi is said to bring good fortune to a new Indian bride. The henna dye is not permanent and usually fades after a few weeks.

people of South Sudan, men paint their bodies with white clay. Originally, the painting was done to make men look menacing in battle. In modern times, they wear the body paint for tribal celebrations. Karo warriors of Ethiopia paint their bodies with white chalk, yellow minerals, black charcoal, and red iron ore to look like the spotted plumage of guinea fowls, a kind of bird. They top off the look with feathers on their heads. In Namibia, Himba women cover their bodies with reddish paint made from ochre—a sign of beauty in their culture.

LONG AGO

Face painting is an ancient art. Historians believe that ancient Egyptians, Assyrians, Babylonians, Indians, Chinese, and others—both men and women—wore makeup. Archaeologists have found ancient cosmetics jars, tubes, and bottles; trays for mixing up makeup; and spoons and sticks for scooping and applying it. The colors came from different minerals: black from manganese oxide, brown from ochre, red from iron oxide and copper, white from lead (which can be poisonous), and blue green from malachite—to name just a few. Colors also came from berries, flowers, henna, and other plants. Queen Cleopatra was said to prefer black makeup on her eyebrows and eye-lashes, blue black on her upper lids, and green on her lower lids.

In many cases, early peoples painted their faces for the same reason many modern people do—to enhance their beauty. But there were other reasons. Certain colors were thought to have magical powers. In ancient India, for example, parents smudged soot around their babies' eyes to protect them from evil spirits. Hindus in India also marked their faces to honor their gods: a U-shaped mark was a sign of devotion to Vishnu (the preserver god of the Hindu trinity), and three horizontal lines stood for Shiva (the destroyer god of the Hindu trinity).

inked

HOW BIG IS THE US TATTOO BUSINESS? WELL, FOR STARTERS, AN ESTIMATED FIFTEEN THOUSAND TATTOO PARLORS OPERATE IN THE UNITED STATES. More than one-third of Americans between the ages of eighteen and twenty-five have tattoos, and about 40 percent of people in the twenty-six to forty age range have tattoos. Television channels overflow with tattoo reality shows, including *Ink Master, Tattoo Age, Tattoo Nightmares, Best Ink, America's Worst Tattoos, Tattoo Highway, LA Ink,* and *Tattoo Wars.*

When it comes to tattoo designs, the sky's the limit. Or more accurately, the *skin's* the limit. Anywhere with skin can have a tattoo. And any mark you can make on paper can be tattooed on your body.

Some people stick to a single image in a single spot. Others combine different images and words to create whole-body masterpieces. In 2011 Californian Julia Gnuse earned the Guinness World Record as the most tattooed woman on Earth. Gnuse, nicknamed the Illustrated Lady, has tattoos on 95 percent of her body, including her face.

ART DEPARTMENT

Popular tattoo designs include stars, crosses, angels, dragons, butterflies, fairies, flowers, hearts, and signs of the zodiac. To find a design they like, some people look at books, such as *The Mammoth Book of Tattoo Art* and the *Tattoo Bible*. If you bring a ready-made design to a tattoo shop, the artist there can transfer it to your skin. If you want a copy of Leonardo da Vinci's *Mona Lisa* tattooed on your back, the artist will do the job. But most tattoo artists are, well, artists—and they love to make their own designs. Some tattoo artists began as commercial illustrators, comic book artists, or graffiti artists before moving to tattoo work.

According to *Guinness World Records*, Isobel Varley *(above)* is the world's most tattooed senior woman. More than two hundred designs cover about three-quarters of her body.

WHAT'S IN A TATTOO?

Tattoos are different from other body art, such as face painting, makeup, and mehndi, because tattoos are meant to be permanent. The tattoo artist uses

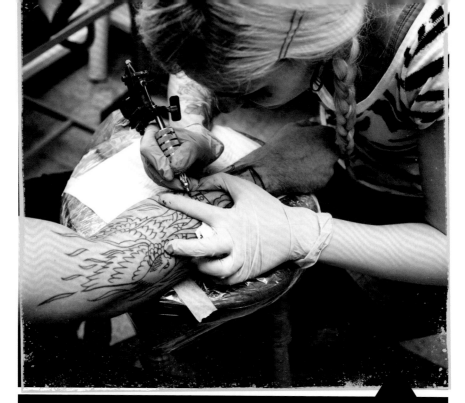

A tattoo machine is a handheld device with needles, used to inject ink into the skin. All reputable tattoo artists wear surgical gloves for medical safety.

an electric machine equipped with one or more needles. The needles inject ink into the dermis layer of skin. (The dermis is below the epidermis, or outer layer.) The ink permanently changes the skin's color. Over time, however, a tattoo will begin to fade. Many people get tattoo touch-ups every few years to keep the colors bright and the lines crisp.

THINK BEFORE YOU INK

What if you tattoo your boyfriend's name on your arm and then decide to dump him? Some people choose a new, darker tattoo over the old one to cover it up. Another option is laser tattoo removal. This process

"RACHEL, WILL YOU MARRY ME?"

–JOE WITTENBURG'S TATTOO MESSAGE TO HIS PARTNER, RACHEL STREETER, 2010

involves using powerful beams of light to break down tattoo ink inside the body. Removing a tattoo with laser light generally takes multiple sessions, spaced several weeks apart.

You can avoid buyer's remorse altogether by choosing temporary tattoos. These decals stick to your skin. A temporary tattoo will stick around for a week or two before it starts to break apart and peel off. You can also remove it at any time you want with body lotion. Another trend is tattoo pantyhose. These sheer pantyhose have flowers, hearts, vines, and other designs. On the wearer's legs, the designs look like tattoos. At the end of the day, when you take off the pantyhose, off come the tattoos.

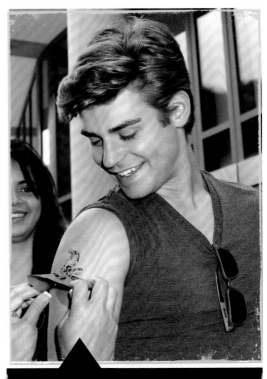

Actor-singer-dancer Garrett Clayton gets a temporary tattoo. You can make your own temporary tattoos with simple materials such as tissue paper and marker pens.

IT'S TRICKY

One awesome tattoo trend is *trompe l'oeil.* That's French for "tricking the eye." Trompe l'oeil tattoos might look like real bracelets on someone's arm, real tears falling down a person's face, real muscles showing through the skin, or a giant spider crawling up someone's neck.

Venezuelan tattoo artist Yomico Moreno wins awards at international tattoo conventions for his trompe l'oeil designs. Another amazing artist is Pavel Arefiev from Russia. His colorful 3-D tattoos leap off the skin!

LONG AGO AND FAR AWAY

We know that ancient people wore tattoos because we have the bodies to prove it. Archaeologists have found mummies with tattoos from Peru, Egypt, and elsewhere. The Pazyryk mummies of central Asia, from a region between Russia and China, are ornately tattooed with images of animals and monsters. The mummies date from around 400 BCE. Tattooed mummies in Peru date to about 1000 CE. Beginning in the 1500s, Spanish conquerors in Mexico, Central America, and South America reported seeing native peoples with tattooed skin.

This hand-colored photo of a tattooed Japanese man dates to the late 1800s. The tattoo tradition in Japan dates back thousands of years. The Japanese word for tattoo is *irezumi*, meaning "to insert ink."

Japan has an ancient tattoo tradition too. Clay figurines from Japanese tombs show that Japanese people were tattooing their bodies as early as 5000 BCE. By the 700s CE, tattoos were a sign of trouble in Japan. As punishment for crimes, people might be tattooed with crosses, lines, circles, and other marks on their faces or arms. A tattoo was a mark of shame—a sign that a person had done something wrong. But in the 1700s, a transition started. Authorities stopped punishing criminals by tattooing. Meanwhile, criminals with penal (punishment) tattoos began covering them over with decorative tattoos. Soon tattoos became a badge of pride for Japanese outlaws. A tattoo was a sign that a man had endured the painful tattooing process. It also was a mark of membership in the rebellious world of organized crime. The tattooing tradition spread to other Japanese tough guys, including firefighters and manual laborers. At the same time, the designs became more and more ornate. They featured pictures of legendary Japanese heroes, religious symbols, animals, flowers, waves, clouds, and lightning bolts. By the early twentieth century, tattooing had become a highly regarded art in Japan. People had their entire backs tattooed, with the pictures continuing onto the arms and down the legs.

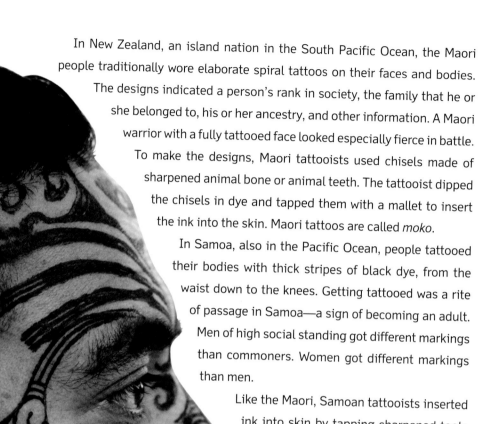

In New Zealand, an island nation in the South Pacific Ocean, the Maori people traditionally wore elaborate spiral tattoos on their faces and bodies. The designs indicated a person's rank in society, the family that he or she belonged to, his or her ancestry, and other information. A Maori warrior with a fully tattooed face looked especially fierce in battle. To make the designs, Maori tattooists used chisels made of sharpened animal bone or animal teeth. The tattooist dipped the chisels in dye and tapped them with a mallet to insert the ink into the skin. Maori tattoos are called *moko*.

In Samoa, also in the Pacific Ocean, people tattooed their bodies with thick stripes of black dye, from the waist down to the knees. Getting tattooed was a rite of passage in Samoa—a sign of becoming an adult. Men of high social standing got different markings than commoners. Women got different markings than men.

Like the Maori, Samoan tattooists inserted ink into skin by tapping sharpened tools with mallets. Samoans and other Pacific Islanders called the tapping process *tatatau*, which means "to tap." European sailors, visiting the islands in the 1700s, changed the name to *tattoo*.

After seeing tattoos in the South Seas, some European sailors wanted their own tattoos. In the 1800s, tattoo

Traditional Maori tattooing is characterized by elegant spirals. Historically, the images were applied using a chisel called an *uhi*. In modern times, a tattoo machine is most commonly used.

artists opened up shop in port cities in Europe and the United States. They decorated the chests, backs, arms, and shoulders of sailors with pictures of ships, anchors, flags, and pretty island women.

For much of the twentieth century, the tattoo trend spread very slowly in the United States. First, sailors and then soldiers got tattoos. Criminals and other tough guys got them, sometimes to show their membership in an outlaw gang. It was unusual to see a woman with a tattoo, however—unless you went to a carnival or a circus. There, you might see a tattooed lady, a sight that was shocking to many Americans. Tattooed ladies were considered circus freaks

An American sailor tattoos a shipmate in this photo from World War II. Sailors were among the first to introduce tattoos to the United States.

INK ON ICE

The oldest tattooed mummy is the Iceman. He was a European who lived more than five thousand years ago. He died in the mountains between Austria and Italy. Soon after, a glacier, or moving ice sheet, covered up his body. The icy cold temperatures kept the body from decaying. When hikers happened upon the Iceman in 1991, he was remarkably well preserved.

Scientists who analyzed the Iceman found fifty-eight small blue-black tattoos, in the form of short lines and crosses, on his legs and back. Some scientists think the tattoos were made for medical purposes. They appear to be acupuncture points, where a healer might have inserted needles to help relieve the Iceman's pain. This theory raises other questions, however. Acupuncture is well documented in ancient China. But it was not known to be practiced in ancient Europe. That leaves the Iceman's tattoos a mystery.

and were displayed along with dwarves, bearded ladies, conjoined twins, and other people with unusual bodies.

In the late 1960s, the hippie movement opened the door for all sorts of unconventional hairstyles and body decoration. The hippie rock and blues singer Janis Joplin wore several tattoos. She paved the way for other young American women to get tattoos. As the twentieth century rolled on, more and more young people got inked. The trend is now a common way for people to express their inner wild!

pierce
IT!

NAME A CELEBRITY—ANY CELEBRITY—AND THAT PERSON PROBABLY HAS AT LEAST ONE PIERCING, PROBABLY MORE. Scarlett Johansson has an eyebrow piercing. Lenny Kravitz has a nostril piercing. Lil Wayne has a lip piercing. Kanye West has an ear piercing. Jessica Alba has a navel piercing.

"NO STORY BEHIND IT. I'M HUMAN . . . AVERAGE LIKE EVERYBODY ELSE. YOU WANT IT, YOU GET IT. I WANTED IT, I GOT IT. . . . I DID IT BECAUSE THIS IS WAYNE AND THIS IS WHAT I WANTED."

—LIL WAYNE, ABOUT A NEW PIERCING, 2008. HE SHOWS OFF HIS DIAMOND TEETH AT RIGHT.

43

Multiple piercings are popular in some parts of the world, including the United States.

You can pierce just about any part of your body. Ever heard of the tragus? It's the little flap of cartilage near your earlobe, just above the opening to your ear. Some people pierce that. Others pierce the nasal septum, the wall between your nostrils. Or they pierce their backs or their tongues or their noses or their eyelids or their private parts.

A piercing is usually just a tiny hole, but shiny bling really shows it off. Belly chains and navel bars are popular. So are studs for tongue piercings, rings for septum piercings, and plugs for ear piercings. Just about any jewelry will do!

THAT'S A STRETCH

In some parts of the world, earplugs are considered pretty cool. To wear this kind of jewelry, you stretch out the earlobes first. That's a gradual process. You start out with a normal ear piercing. After wearing an ordinary stud for a few weeks, you switch to a cone-shaped plug called an ear taper. That stretches the lobe a little bit more. After a few more weeks, you switch to a bigger taper and on and on until your earlobe is stretched as big as you want it to go. All sorts of awesome jewelry—colorful plugs, rings, curly tapers, and straight tapers—are out there to fill the hole in your earlobe.

Ear stretching might sound like the latest piercing trend, but the practice isn't new at all. Inca sculptures show noblemen wearing enormous round earplugs hundreds of years ago. In many places, ear stretching has continued into modern times. In Southeast Asia, for instance, Hmong women stretch out their ears starting in childhood. By the time they are grown, they can fit huge hollow rings in their earlobes. Tribal peoples wear similar styles in Ethiopia and other parts of Africa and in the Amazon region of Brazil.

Ear stretching is a decorative practice that originated among indigenous peoples across the globe. Natural materials such as bone, wood, and stone were used and are still common for earplugs. This young Suri woman is from southern Ethiopia.

I'VE GOT YOU UNDER MY SKIN

Some people like their bling so much that they have it permanently affixed to their skin. In a process called transdermal implanting, a stud or other decorative piece is implanted into the skin. You can see the jewelry on the outside of the skin, but you don't see the anchor that holds it in place beneath the skin. Baseball player Covelli Loyce "Coco" Crisp has a stud implanted into his neck.

American baseball player Coco Crisp got a lot of media attention in 2011 when he first sported a combination tattoo and neck implant.

With a different procedure, subdermal implanting, objects are placed beneath the skin entirely. For instance, someone might have a row of beads implanted beneath the skin. On the outside, you wouldn't see the beads, but you would see raised bumps where the beads are. People achieve all sorts of interesting bumps and shapes by implanting objects beneath their skin. Examples include stars, doughnuts, rings, scrolls, and skulls.

HORNS

In 2011 Lady Gaga appeared on *The Jay Leno Show* with four hornlike bumps—one above and one below each eye. Rumors flew that she had subdermal implants. But the next time she appeared on TV, the bumps were gone. Apparently, her makeup artist had only glued them on for the show. Had Gaga had real implants, she would have undergone a short surgical procedure involving cutting into the skin, inserting the objects, and then having the skin stitched up around

'ROUND THE WORLD

Piercing, stretching, cutting, and changing the shape of various body parts all fall under the category of body modification. US traditions of body modification are fairly tame compared to other parts of the world.

Consider this: In the Sepik region of Papua New Guinea, male elders make a series of cuts on the arms, chests, and backs of younger men as part of a coming-of-age ritual. The wounds are treated with wood smoke, oil, and clay, which cause the cuts to swell. The wounds then heal into a series of raised bumps that look like crocodile skin. Someone who undergoes this ritual is called a Crocodile Man and is respected for his strength and courage.

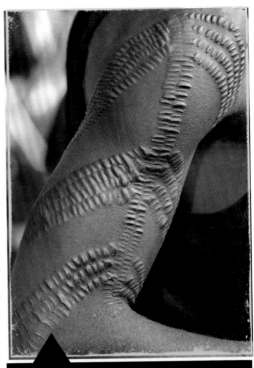

Scarification is common among the Pokot people of eastern Africa. After cutting patterns into the skin, charcoal or plant sap is rubbed into the fresh cuts to cause intentional scarring.

SCAR TISSUE

In parts of Africa, some people practice scarification—the intentional scarring of the skin by cutting or burning—to show their strength and courage. Scarification in parts of West Africa, for example, is a tribal ritual associated with puberty and marriage. In the United States, scarification was historically used in a horrific way, to brand slaves or to punish criminals. In modern times, some Americans use scarification to make designs, words, or pictures in the skin to express creativity or personal beliefs. The practice is also popular in Japan.

Among the Padaung people in the Southeast Asian nation of Burma (also called Myanmar), a long neck is a sign of feminine beauty. As young as the age of two, Padaung girls start wearing heavy brass coils around their necks. Gradually, over years, more and more coils are added. The weight of the coils presses down on a girl's shoulders and collarbone and makes her neck appear longer. Adult Padaung women usually wear twenty coils around their necks. Because the coils weaken the neck muscles, women can't hold up their heads without them.

Among the Mursi people of Ethiopia, women stretch out their lower lips with wooden or clay discs. When her lip is fully stretched out, a Mursi girl is considered a woman and is ready for marriage. In the Amazon River region of South America, among the Kayapo people, it is the men who wear lip plates. These plates are a sign of strength and manhood.

This young Padaung woman wears more than a dozen neck coils. Ndebele women of southern Africa once commonly wore brass or copper neck rings too. They now often wear layers of beads to give the impression of having very long necks.

LONG AGO

We know for sure that people in ancient Asia pierced their ears. An Iranian figurine from about 3000 BCE shows a woman with four piercings in each ear. A wall mural from ancient China shows a woman with big heavy earrings that have stretched out her earlobes. Statues of the Siddhartha Gautama, an ancient Indian philosopher who founded the Buddhist religion, often show him with long stretched-out earlobes, indicating that he probably wore earrings or earplugs. Archaeologists have also found many ancient earrings themselves, including gold hoops from ancient Cyprus and earplugs from ancient Guatemala. The piercing tra-

World-renowned English playwright William Shakespeare (1564–1616) wore an ear piercing.

dition continued up through the Middle Ages and into more recent times. Some European pirates wore earrings, and the British playwright William Shakespeare wore one too. By the twentieth century, people were piercing every body part imaginable.

Piercing and other body modification might be old practices, but they're clearly here to stay. That guy down the street with a big ring through his nose is just carrying on a tradition of the ancients. Whether you're in the Amazon, Africa, or Anytown USA, the names and faces might change, but body decoration lives on.

VISUAL GLOSSARY

What does it mean? Using what you've learned in this book, see if you and your friends can determine the methods and the significance behind each of the following examples of body art. Discuss how you figured out each one and what the clues were. Were some harder to figure out than others? Why or why not? Do some research online to see if you can come up with other examples.

SOURCE NOTES

8   Soulja Boy, *BrainyQuote*, "Soulja Boy Quotes," accessed April 17, 2013, http://www
    .brainyquote.com/quotes/authors/s/soulja_boy.html.

15 *Teen Vogue*, "10 Questions with Nicki Minaj," accessed April 16, 2013, http://www
    .teenvogue.com/celebrity-style/2011-04/nicki-minaj-interview/?slide=1.

20 Richard Corson, *Fashions in Hair: The First Five Thousand Years* (London: Peter Owen, 2001),
    19.

23 Lauren Paxman, "I Sometimes Even Forget They're There' (But Driving Can Be a Bit of a
    Problem): Singer Who Hasn't Cut Her Nails for 18 Years," *DailyMailOnline,* November 28,
    2011, http://www.dailymail.co.uk/femail/article-2067169/Chris-Walton-fingernails-Singer-
    recognised-having-worlds-longest-nails.html.

27 *Gaga Media*, "Lady Gaga Interviewed by *Stylist* Magazine, Reveals New ARTPOP Track,"
    October 31, 2012, http://gagamedia.net/?p=9744.

36 *Huff Post*, "Man Proposes Marriage with Tattoo," July 26, 2010, http://www.huffingtonpost
    .com/2010/05/26/man-proposes-marriage-wit_n_590475.html.

43 *Hip Hop Lead*, "Lil Wayne: Talks of His New Piercing Boring Rappers," November 3, 2008,
    http://www.hiphoplead.com/news/lil-wayne-talks-of-his-new-piercing-and-about-not-
    been-excited-with-the/.

SELECTED BIBLIOGRAPHY

"A Brief History of Tattoos." *Designboom*. Accessed March 3, 2013. http://www.designboom.com/
    history/tattoo_history.html.

Corson, Richard. *Fashions in Hair: The First Five Thousand Years*. 9th ed. London: Peter Owen,
    2001.

———. *Fashions in Makeup: From Ancient to Modern Times*. Rev. ed. London: Peter Owen, 2003.

"A History of Japanese Tattooing." *Vanishing Tattoo*. Accessed March 3, 2013. http://www
    .vanishingtattoo.com/tattoo_museum/chinese_japanese_tattoos.html.

"History of Nail Polish." *Popular Nail Polish*. Last modified November 2009. http://www
    .popularnailpolish.blogspot.com/2009/11/history-of-nail-polish.html.

Jones, Catherine Cartwright. "Henna and Fingernails." *The Encyclopedia of Henna*. Accessed
    March 3, 2013. http://www.hennapage.com/henna/encyclopedia/fingernails/.

Mack, John, ed. *Ethnic Jewelry*. Burlington, VT: Lund Humphries, 2002.

Paglia, Camille. *Glittering Images: A Journey through Art from Egypt to Star Wars*. New York:
    Pantheon Books, 2012.

Rush, John A. *Spiritual Tattoo: A Cultural History of Tattooing, Piercing, Scarification, Branding,
    and Implants*. Berkeley, CA: Frog, 2005.

Savacool, Julia. "Hairstyles from around the World." *Marie Claire*, April 23, 2007. http://www
    .marieclaire.com/world-reports/news/hairstyles-world.

"Tattoos." *Samoan Sensation*. Last modified April 21, 2000. http://www.samoa.co.uk/tattoos.html.

Tait, Hugh, ed. *Jewelry: Seven Thousand Years*. New York: Harry N. Abrams, 1991.

Trumble, Angus. *The Finger: A Handbook*. New York: Farrar, Straus and Giroux, 2010.

WinStar Productions. *Body Art*. DVD. New York: Wellspring Media, 2000.

FURTHER INFORMATION

BOOKS

Andrich, Tom. *Decorate Yourself: Cool Designs for Temporary Tattoos, Face Painting, Henna and More*. New York: Sterling/Tamos, 2003. This book provides step-by-step instructions for decorating your face, body, and nails with temporary tattoos, henna patterns, and body paint.

Currie-McGhee, L. K. *Tattoos and Body Piercing*. Detroit: Lucent, 2005. This title explores the reasons people get tattoos and body piercings and explores associated health and legal issues.

Drew, Sarah. *Junk-Box Jewelry: 25 DIY Low Cost (or No Cost) Jewelry Projects*. San Francisco: Zest Books, 2012. This illustrated book for teens shows you how to make jewelry from found and recycling objects, including pebbles, fabric scraps, screws, and washers.

Krull, Kathleen. *Big Wig: A Little History of Hair*. New York: Arthur A. Levine Books, 2011. Krull presents fascinating information on hair fashions, starting at the dawn of history and bringing readers into contemporary times.

Levy, Janey. *Tattoos in Modern Society*. New York: Rosen, 2008. This title looks at tattooing and how this once traditional practice has become mainstream, both in the United States and worldwide.

Miller, Jean-Chris. *The Body Art Book: A Complete Illustrated Guide to Tattoos, Piercings, and Other Body Modifications*. St. Louis: Turtleback Books, 2004. This title explores tattooing, piercing, and other body modification practices, with advice about safety, care, and removal of body art. The author is the editorial director for several tattooing publications.

Nagle, Jeanne. *Why People Get Tattoos and Other Body Art*. New York: Rosen, 2012. This resource investigates the top cultural and anthropological reasons people practice the art of tattooing and proudly display tattoos. Readers learn about the roles of tattoos in religion, ritual, cultural identity, and more.

Roleff, Tamara. *Body Piercing and Tattoos*. Detroit: Greenhaven, 2007. This book contains a diverse collection of personal narratives about body piercing and tattoos.

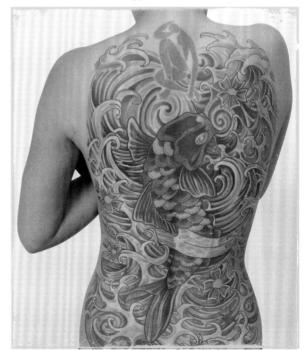

FURTHER INFORMATION CONTINUED

Tait, Hugh, ed. *7000 Years of Jewelry*. Buffalo: Firefly Books, 2008. This book, edited by a British Museum expert on the history of jewelry, explores jewelry in civilizations around the globe. Among the many masterpieces highlighted in the book are Egyptian necklaces, Celtic torcs (neck rings), South American gold masks, Renaissance pendants, and Art Nouveau buckles. The book includes hundreds of high-quality photos.

Tolliver, Gabriel, and Reggie Osse. *Bling: The Hip-Hop Jewelry Book*. New York: Bloomsbury USA, 2006. This book takes a dazzling look at the history of bling in the hip-hop world, with interesting facts about jewels, the performers who wear them, and much more.

WEBSITES

Bodies of Cultures
http://www.penn.museum/sites/body_modification/bodmodintro.shtml
This site from the University of Pennsylvania Museum of Archaeology and Anthropology provides an overview of piercing, tattooing, and body painting through history, with links to examples from the museum's collections.

History of Jewellery
http://www.vam.ac.uk/content/articles/h/jewellery-through-the-ages/
This web page from London's acclaimed Victoria and Albert Museum traces the history of jewelry from ancient to modern times.

Nail Art Gallery
nailartgallery.nailsmag.com
At this website from *Nails* magazine, people post pictures of their own nail art. You can see hundreds of examples of fantastic nail art and also learn how to make nail art yourself.

Skin Stories: The Art and Culture of Polynesian Tattoos
http://www.pbs.org/skinstories/history/index.html
Tattooing has a long history in the islands of the Pacific Ocean. This website from the Public Broadcasting System explores the history and culture of tattooing in Samoa, Hawaii, and New Zealand.

Virtual Hairstyle and Makeup Makeover
http://www.marieclaire.com/hair-beauty/trends/virtual-hairstyle-makeovers
At this website from *Marie Claire* magazine, you can upload your own photo and give yourself a virtual hair and makeup makeover. See what you'd look like with long red hair, sparkly pink lips, and smoky green eyes. The options are endless.

World Beard and Moustache Championships
http://www.worldbeardchampionships.com
Learn about extreme facial hair and the men who compete for awards at the yearly competition.

World Body Painting Festival
http://www.bodypainting-festival.com/en/
This yearly festival in Austria brings together artists, photographers, and models to celebrate the art of body painting. The event includes workshops, awards, and a "body circus."

INDEX

ABOUT THE AUTHOR

Stephen G. Gordon was born in Cleveland, Ohio, and graduated from Kent State University. He makes his home in northern New Mexico, where he writes about sports, music, art, and culture.

PHOTO ACKNOWLEDGMENTS

The images in this book are used with the permission of: © Kornilovdream/Dreamstime.com, p. 1; © Jun Sato/WireImage/Getty Images, p. 5 (left); © Isis and Nefertari, from the Tomb of Nefertari, New Kingdom (mural), Egyptian 19th Dynasty (c.1297-1185 BC)/Valley of the Queens, Thebes, Egypt/Giraudon/The Bridgeman Art Library, p. 5 (right); © iStockphoto. com/iconogenic, p. 6; © Dave J Hogan/Getty Images, pp. 7, 22; © Mark Davis/Getty Images for TV Guide, p. 8; © Hilary Morgan/Alamy, p. 9; © Narinder Nanu/AFP/Getty Images, p. 11; Album/Oronoz/Newscom, p. 13; Matt Sayles/Invision/AP Photo, p. 14; © WIN-Initiative/ Getty Images, p. 15; © Stryjerk/Dreamstime.com, p. 16; AP Photo/PA, Clara Molden, p. 17; © Peter Adams/JAI/CORBIS, p. 18; © Hugh Sitton/CORBIS, p. 19; © Hung Meng Tan/ Dreamstime.com, p. 21; © Stan Honda/AFP/Getty Images, p. 23; © Yoshikazu Tsuno/ AFP/Getty Images, p. 24; © Bruno Morandi/CORBIS, p. 25; © Venturelli/WireImage/Getty Images, p. 27; © Jason Merritt/WireImages/Getty Images, p. 28; IDF/Chameleons eye/Rafeel Ben-Ari/Newscom, p. 29; © Marc Anderson/Alamy, p. 31; © Image Source/Getty Images, p. 32; © iStockphoto/Thinkstock, p. 34; Eloy Alonso/Reuters/Newscom, p. 35; © iStockphoto. com/Jose Juan Garcia, p. 36; © Tibrina Hobson/WireImage/Getty Images, p. 37; © SSPL/ Getty Images, p. 39; © Tim Graham/The Image Bank/Getty Images, p. 40; © MPI/Stringer/ Archive Photos/Getty Images, p. 41; © Ronald Martinez/Getty Images, p. 43; © Lamada/ Vetta/Getty Images, p. 44; © Eric Lafforgue/Alamy, p. 45; Mike Stone/Reuters/Newscom, p. 46; © Nigel Pavitt/JAI/CORBIS, p. 47; © Chris Hammond Photography/Alamy, p. 48; © Portrait of William Shakespeare (1564-1616) c.1610 (oil on canvas), Taylor, John (d. 1651) (attr. to)/National Portrait Gallery, London, UK/The Bridgeman Art Library, p. 49; © CORBIS, p. 50 (left); © Martin Bureau/AFP/Getty Images, p. 50 (right); © Fred Duval/FilmMagic/ Getty Images, p. 51 (top); © Charles & Josette Lenars/CORBIS, p. 51 (bottom left); © Michael Ochs Archives/Stringer/Getty Images, p. 51 (bottom right); © Todd Strand/Independent Picture Service, p. 53.

Front cover: © iStockphoto.com/Oktay Ortakcioglu.